Cherished Teddies™

Angels Among Us

Heavenly Messages
of Love

Publications International, Ltd.

©1998 Priscilla Hillman.
Licensed by Enesco Corporation, owner
of the CHERISHED TEDDIES trademark.

Quotations on pages 11 (bottom), 16 (bottom), 28 (bottom), 44 (top), and 46 written by Priscilla Hillman, artist and creator of the Cherished Teddies™ collection. Other quotations compiled and written by Kelly Womer, a freelance writer whose work has appeared in several national collectibles publications.

Photography by Brian Warling.

Photo styling by Lisa Wright.

Acknowledgments:
Page 19: Excerpt from *Among Angels*, copyright © 1995 by Nancy Willard and Jane Yolen, reprinted by permission of Harcourt Brace & Company.
Page 20: Excerpt from *Angel Letters*, © 1991 by Sophy Burnham, reprinted by permission of Ballantine Books, a division of Random House, Inc.

Copyright © 1998 Publications International, Ltd. All rights reserved. This book may not be reproduced or quoted in whole or in part by any means whatsoever without written permission from:

Louis Weber, C.E.O.
Publications International, Ltd.
7373 North Cicero Avenue
Lincolnwood, Illinois 60646

Permission is never granted for commercial purposes.

Manufactured in China.

8 7 6 5 4 3 2 1

ISBN: 0-7853-2930-7

ANGELS AMONG US

*An angel of compassion
is like a bowl of
chicken soup made by Mom.
It makes you feel all warm inside.
It makes you feel loved.*

*Every time you meet
a stranger, it's also
a chance to make a friend... and
perhaps be touched by an angel.*

ANGELS AMONG US

Lullaby and goodnight,
thy mother's delight,
fair angels above
will guard thee in love;
They will keep thee from harm,
Thou shalt wake in my arms.

— Johannes Brahms

ANGELS AMONG US

ANGELS AMONG US

ANGELS AMONG US

*A little cherub
sings with joy
For every baby girl and boy.
Flying by their side always,
Celebrating all their days.*

*True friendship is a knot that
angel hands have tied.*

—Anonymous

ANGELS AMONG US

ANGELS AMONG US

Be my Teddie Bear Angel
Be there to snuggle
Be there to hug
Be there to love
Be there to comfort
Be there always.

My teddy bear is stuffed with love and happy memories.

—Priscilla Hillman

ANGELS AMONG US

Each star in the sky is an angel who glows with a brilliant radiance and shines as a beacon of hope in the darkness.

*Nourish your body
Enlighten your mind
Refresh your soul
And you will feel as light as an angel gliding through the sky.*

ANGELS AMONG US

ANGELS AMONG US

ANGELS AMONG US

*A bouquet of flowers says
"I love you."
A cooing dove says
"Peace be with you."
A tender hug says "I care for you."
A guardian angel says "I am always
with you."*

ANGELS AMONG US

The angel on your shoulder whispers in your ear: "You are loved, so love others. You are blessed, so bless others. You are my friend, so be a friend."

A teddie bear's real charm is in being huggable.

— Priscilla Hillman

ANGELS AMONG US

ANGELS AMONG US

ANGELS AMONG US

*Angels fly
because
they take themselves
lightly above
the gravity
of any situation.*

*Angels fly
because
they take themselves
lightly.*

—Jane Yolen

ANGELS AMONG US

They play with us. They look after us. They heal us, touch us, comfort us with invisible warm hands, and always they try to give us what we want.

—Sophy Burnham

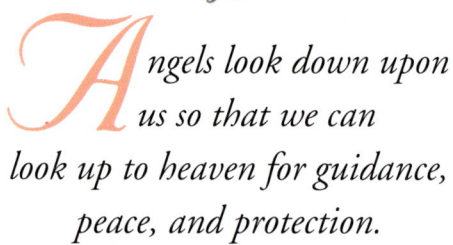

Angels look down upon us so that we can look up to heaven for guidance, peace, and protection.

ANGELS AMONG US

ANGELS AMONG US

ANGELS AMONG US

*May the angel of happiness
flutter into your
life each day like a butterfly that
rises from its cocoon to spread its
colorful wings for the first time.*

*Put on your halo every day
to be a blessing to others
and to share small kindnesses with
those you pass along your way.*

ANGELS AMONG US

Certainly angels have a sense of humor. How else could they keep their feathers from getting ruffled? How else could they wear halos that never stay on straight? How else could they make us smile and feel all happy inside?

ANGELS AMONG US

Angels Among Us

Angels Among Us

Angels help us believe in those things we can't see and understand things we can. Angels give us the gift of faith and wisdom to know all things are possible.

ANGELS AMONG US

The angel of the morning wakes the sun from its slumber to greet the new day. The angel of the evening lulls the sun to sleep.

One can resist temptation, but not a teddie bear.

—Priscilla Hillman

Angels Among Us

ANGELS AMONG US

ANGELS AMONG US

Everyone who performs a good deed is truly an angel. For one doesn't need to wear feathered wings or golden halos to offer a heavenly helping hand.

ANGELS AMONG US

*Charity is an angel who
looks for those in need
And then shares grace and
kindness in word and deed.
She may never show her
face or reveal her name,
But her acts of generosity are
special all the same.*

ANGELS AMONG US

ANGELS AMONG US

*Listen to the sparrow's song.
It's soft and serene
like a breeze whistling through the
woods or the gurgling of a brook.
It's an angelic song that resonates
with heaven's voice.*

ANGELS AMONG US

Angels Among Us

ANGELS AMONG US

A teddie bear is an angel with open fluffy arms instead of feathered wings for giving hugs and sparkling button eyes instead of a halo to shine with love.

ANGELS AMONG US

Whenever you take a journey—whether across town to a familiar home or across the country to a new place— remember to take an angel with you. The angel will guide your path, watch your steps, and keep you company all along the way.

ANGELS AMONG US

ANGELS AMONG US

There's a little angel in all of us wanting to make a big difference in the lives of others. Set that little angel free and the world will be a better place because of you.

ANGELS AMONG US

ANGELS AMONG US

Angels Among Us

An angel doesn't have to speak to be heard, be visible to be seen, or be present to be felt. Believe in angels, and they will always be near.

ANGELS AMONG US

Why do people love teddie bears? Because they don't eat much, never betray a secret, never swear, and never, never steal all the covers.

— Priscilla Hillman

Walking with an angel is a step of faith— and a journey that lasts a lifetime.

Angels Among Us

45

ANGELS AMONG US

Prescription for the common cold: rest, plenty of Mom's homemade chicken soup, and one sympathetic teddie bear.

—Priscilla Hillman